THE 100

MOST

TRADITIONAL

CHINESE CHARACTERS

www.royalcollins.com

THE 100 MOST

MOST

TRADITIONAL
CHINESE CHARACTERS

XU HUI

TRANSLATED BY JULIE LOO

 Chemical Industry Press

THE 100 MOST TRADITIONAL CHINESE CHARACTERS

Xu Hui
Translated by Julie Loo

First published in 2022 by Royal Collins Publishing Group Inc.
Groupe Publication Royal Collins Inc.
BKM Royalcollins Publishers Private Limited

Headquarters: 550-555 boul. René-Lévesque O Montréal (Québec) H2Z1B1 Canada
India office: 805 Hemkunt House, 8th Floor, Rajendra Place, New Delhi 110008

Original Edition © Chemical Industry Press

ISBN: 978-1-4878-0772-6

To find out more about our publications, please visit www.royalcollins.com.

As well as its obvious visual appeal, China's millennia-old writing system is a carrier of the nation's culture and identity. In this book, Xu Hui selects and explains the 100 most traditional Chinese characters with the help of eye-catching illustrations that bring their meanings alive, and historic tracings through seal script all the way back to ancient oracle bone carvings. For novices and experts alike, this translation by Julie Loo offers English readers a compelling insight into the world of written Chinese.

 person, scholar [shì]

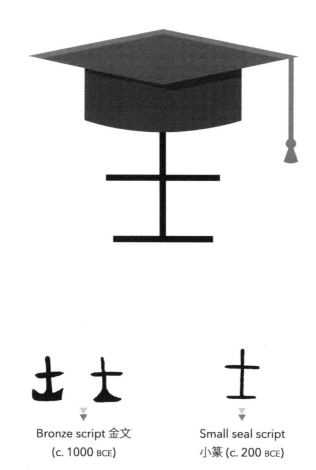

Bronze script 金文
(c. 1000 BCE)

Small seal script
小篆 (c. 200 BCE)

- 士 was used to address men, because men were responsible for the most important things.
- Confucius' explanation for 士 was pushing 十 [shí] *ten* to combine with 一 [yī] *one*, carrying the idea of being very knowledgeable.
- 女士 [nǚ shì] *lady* was not a borrowed phrase from a foreign language. Its earliest appearance was in *Shijing (The Classic of Poetry)*.
- The initial idea of 绅士 [shēn shì] was not the same as 'gentleman' in the West. It actually referred to the stratum of scholars who were required to wear belts that were three feet long.

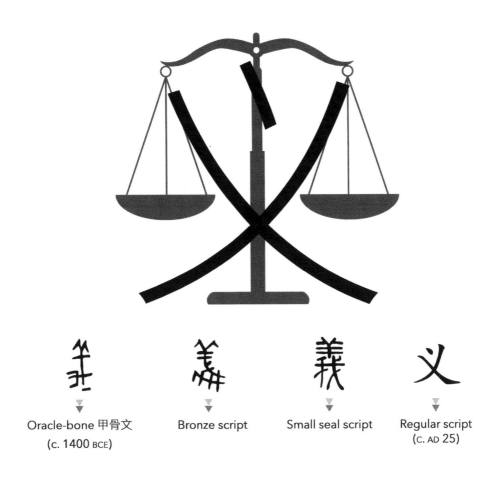

| Oracle-bone 甲骨文 (c. 1400 BCE) | Bronze script | Small seal script | Regular script (C. AD 25) |

- The oracle bone script for this character was an associative compound or a compound ideograph. It featured a goat above a weapon, carrying the idea of appropriate moral ethics, actions, or reasons. The overall notion was *righteousness*.
- In ancient times, the characters 义 and 谊 [yì] *friendship* were used interchangeably. In the cases of 无情无义 [wú qíng wú yì] *heartless* and 忘恩负义 [wàng ēn fù yì] *ungratefulness*, the character 义 refers to 情谊 [qíng yì] *friendly sentiments*.

 bifurcated, forked [yā]

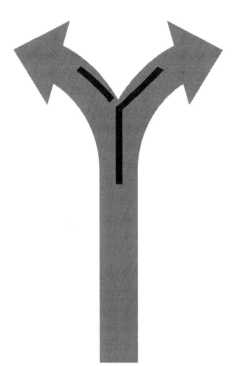

丫

Small seal script

Hair style of maids in Tang Dynasty

- In earlier times, this character referred to things that were bifurcated.
- 丫鬟 [yā huán] *servant girl* was originally written as 鴉鬟 [yā huán]. Due to the common hairstyle of a young girl, the name 丫头 [yā tou] was used to address her.
- During the Tang Dynasty, the name 丫头 was a laudatory title for a young girl.
- 丫鬟 also referred to young girls who had not yet married.
- During the Song Dynasty, the two phrases 丫头 and 丫鬟 were used to mean *slave girls* or *servant girls*.

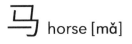 horse [mǎ]

Oracle-bone

Bronze script

Small seal script

马

Regular script

- People in ancient times believed that the horse was the spirit of the earth (ground). It possessed internal heat, and was a military beast.
- During the Tang Dynasty, the phrase 毛病 [máo bing] *trouble, illness, disease* was used to mean that the color of a horse's hair was not good.
- The horse ranked top among domesticated animals. Since it was the biggest, people of old began to use the character 马 to refer to things that were huge. 马路 [mǎ lù] was therefore a large road, not a dirt road for horses to travel on.

 corpse [shī]

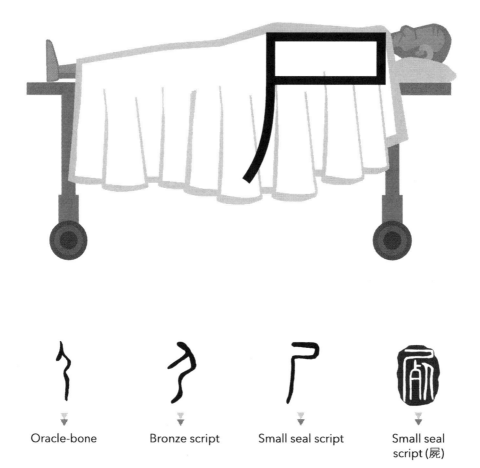

| Oracle-bone | Bronze script | Small seal script | Small seal script (屍) |

- The character 尸 appeared before 屍 [shī]. Either character could be used to denote *a dead body*.
- The original idea behind 尸 was living people representing the dead to accept sacrificial offerings during ritual ceremonies.
- 尸位 [shī wèi] *to hold a job without doing a stroke of work* originally referred to the descendants of the dead accepting sacrifices on their behalf during sacrificial rites. These people were not required to do anything during the ceremony. Eventually, this situation gave rise to the phrase 尸位素餐 [shī wèi sù cān] *taking up a place and eating food but not contributing.*
- During sacrificial ceremonies, 尸 must not be confused with 屍.

尤 outstanding [yóu]

Oracle-bone   Bronze script   Small seal script

- In ancient times, 尤物 [yóu wù] *bewitching female beauty* referred to a wanton woman who used her beauty to entice men and bring about their downfall. Men with strong morals and ethics would stay away from such women.
- Only with sublime moral conduct could a man withstand the temptation of a 尤物.
- 尤物 was previously used to mean *outstanding people*.
- 尤 is related to 疣 [yóu], which means *sarcoma*.

中 middle [zhōng]

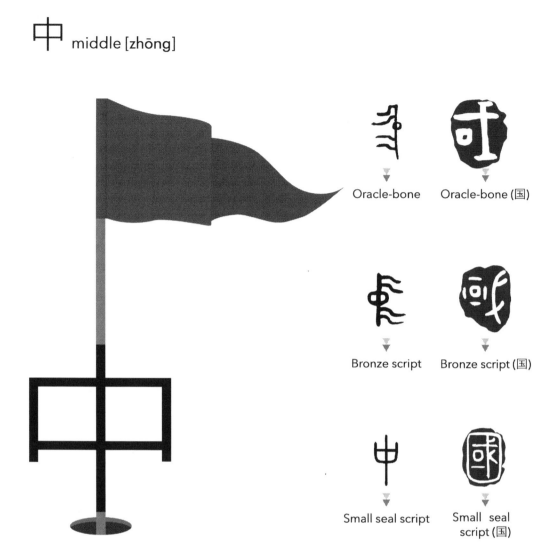

Oracle-bone

Oracle-bone (国)

Bronze script

Bronze script (国)

Small seal script

Small seal script (国)

- This character initially referred to a flag.
- 建中 [jiàn zhōng] refers to placing an army's flag in the middle of an area of land.
- Initially, the phrase 中国 [zhōng guó] *China* referred to Luoyang as the center of the Central Plains.
- The phrase 中国 can also refer to the capital of a country.

 book [shū]

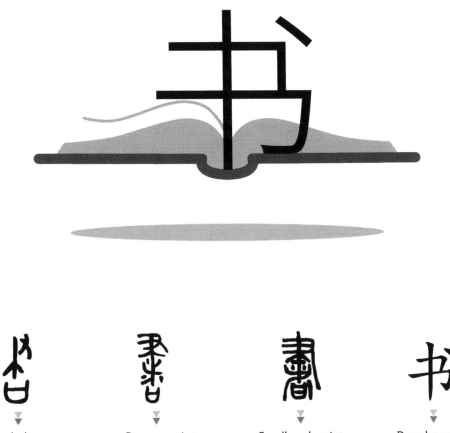

甲	甲	甲	书
▼	▼	▼	▼
Oracle-bone	Bronze script	Small seal script	Regular script

- The oracle bone script for this character was an associative compound. It resembled a hand holding a brush, denoting the idea of writing.
- People in ancient times placed herbs between books to prevent damage from silverfish. This gave rise to the phrase 书香 [shū xiāng] *a literary family*.
- The herb that was used to keep silverfish at bay was 芸 [yún] *rue*. Subsequently, intellectuals in ancient times used the phrases 芸帙 [yún yì] and 芸编 [yún biān] to mean *books*.

玉 jade [yù]

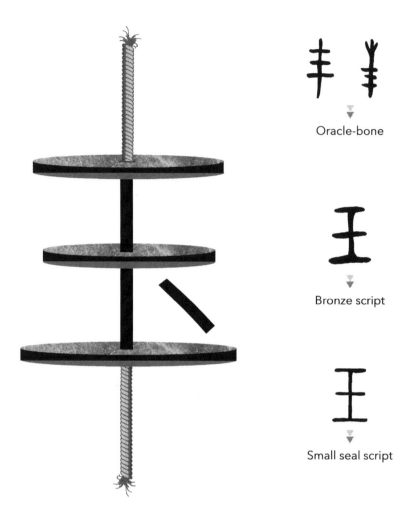

Oracle-bone

Bronze script

Small seal script

- In ancient times, jade was comparable to a man of noble character. It possessed five moral integrities – benevolence, righteousness, wisdom, courage, and purity.
- Ancient etiquette stipulated that a man of noble character must wear a jade ornament.
- 玉体 [yù tǐ] *body* does not necessarily denote femaleness. It was a respectful term to address another person's body.
- In ancient times, sacrificial offerings, diplomatic affairs, and social activities had strict rules regarding the types of jade ornaments that were to be used. No mistakes were allowed.

 东 east [dōng]

 Oracle-bone Bronze script Small seal script Regular script

- This is a compound ideographic character. It resembled a tree standing in the middle of the sun, indicating the direction of the sunrise.
- The tree in the middle of the character was the mythical 若木 [ruò mù]. It was also called 扶桑 [fú sāng] *a large mulberry*. It grew in the extreme east. Subsequently, Japan was also called the country of 扶桑.
- According to ancient etiquette, 东 represented the seat of the host. This gave rise to such phrases as 东家 [dōng jiā] *master*, and 房东 [fáng dōng] *landlord*.

左 left [zuǒ]

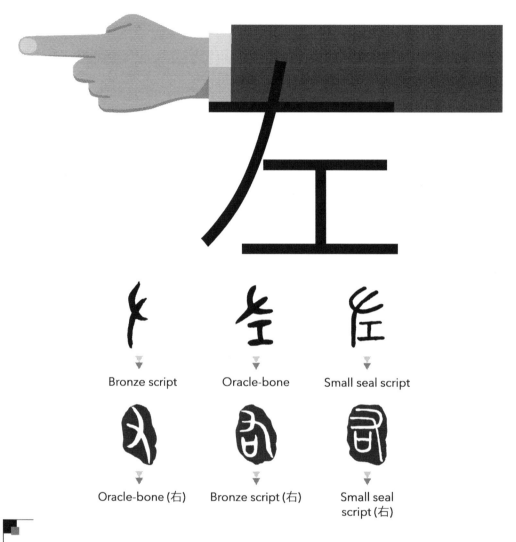

Bronze script   Oracle-bone   Small seal script

Oracle-bone (右)   Bronze script (右)   Small seal script (右)

- The character 左 was originally written as 佐, meaning *to assist*.
- 右 [yòu] was initially written as 又. The semantic 口 [kǒu] was added later to distinguish it.
- In ancient times, right and left symbolized status. Right was for the honored, and left was for the lowly.
- The emperor would sit facing the south. Thus, in geography, the east was on the left, while the west was on the right. However, on modern-day maps, this direction is the exact opposite.

归 to return [guī]

| Oracle-bone | Bronze script | Small seal script | Regular script |

— The original idea of this character was the marriage of a woman.

— 来归 [lái guī] referred to a married woman who was stripped of her status by her husband's family, and had to return to her parents' home.

— The medicinal herb 当归 [dāng guī] *angelica* can improve blood circulation. It is an important remedy in the treatment of female health problems. The name was derived from a woman's longing for her husband's 归来 [guī lái] *return*.

处 department, place, part [chù] / to dwell, to live, to be situated in [chǔ]

Bronze script   Small seal script   Regular script

- The complex character 處 originated from 处. It could be considered as a compound ideograph in its metal script form. It denoted the idea of a person leaning on something as if to rest.
- The idea of 处 was *to discontinue, to stop*. A nobleman who chose to stay at home as a recluse was known as 处士 [chǔ shì] or 处子 [chǔ zǐ] *a person who is not yet of age*.
- In ancient times, girls who had not married were called 处女 [chǔ nǚ] *virgin*. The character 处 should be read with the third tone.

瓜 melon [guā]

Bronze script   Small seal script

– 瓜代 [guā dài] referred to *the change of personnel between terms of service.* Originally, the change of personnel was carried out during the period when the melons were ripe.
– The character 瓜 in the phrase 傻瓜 [shǎ guā] *fool* does not refer to a melon.
– 破瓜 [pò guā] *to deflower a virgin* used to refer to sixteen-year-old girls. It was later used in novels to describe the deflowering of a girl.

礼 ceremony, gift, etiquette, courtesy [lǐ]

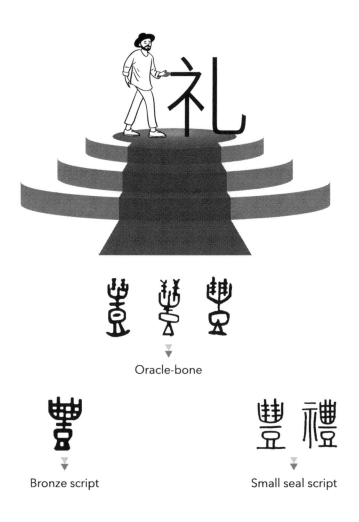

Oracle-bone

Bronze script   Small seal script

- The complex character 禮 came from the character 豊. It consisted of a dish stand filled with food, above the character 豆 [dòu] *bean*.
- 礼 was considered the same as 履 [lǚ] *to fulfil*, denoting the idea of carrying out rites and etiquette.
- People in ancient times put 礼 on a pedestal. It became an organized way to manage the whole patriarchal hierarchy system.
- Today, the significance of 礼 has been reduced to mean *manners and etiquette for interpersonal relationships.*

 mother [mǔ]

Oracle-bone

Bronze script

Small seal script

- This is a pictographic character showing a person kneeling, hands on waist and breasts on the chest.
- Calling a birthday 母难日 [mǔ nán rì] *the day when the mother had to go through the excruciating pain of childbirth* started as early as the Yuan Dynasty.
- Before the Tang Dynasty, Chinese people did not celebrate birthdays. Instead, they had to fast to show gratitude to their parents.
- People in ancient times considered the thumb as the base of the five fingers. Thus, its name contains the character 母.

寺 temple, government bureau in ancient China [sì]

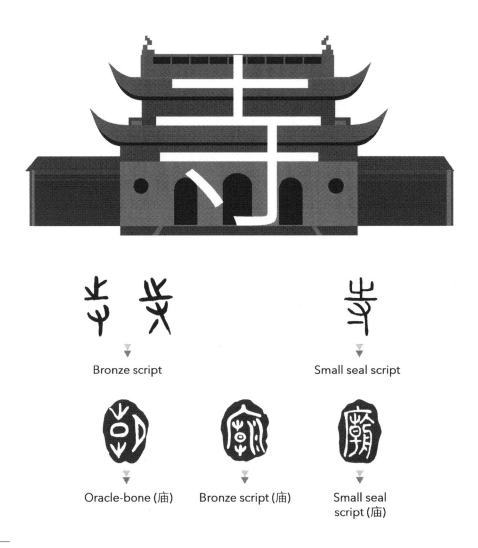

Bronze script

Small seal script

Oracle-bone (庙)

Bronze script (庙)

Small seal
script (庙)

- Before the Jin Dynasty, 寺 and 庙 [miào] *temple, shrine* were two different places. They were not used interchangeably.
- 寺 originally referred to the law, indicating government offices. It wasn't until the Eastern Han Dynasty that the character was used to denote a Buddhist temple.
- 庙 originally referred to an ancestral shrine, meant for the sacrificial worship of ancestors.
- By the end of the Western Jin Dynasty, the two characters were used interchangeably as the general names for Buddhist temples.

 net, network [wǎng]

Oracle-bone	Bronze script	Small seal script	Regular script

- This is a pictographic character. It resembled a net held in place on the ground by two rods.
- People in ancient times were specific with their classification. Nets for fishing were known as 罟 [gǔ] *fishing net*. Nets for birds and other animals were known as 网.
- More specifically, 网 was used to catch animals. 罗 [luó] was used to catch birds. The combined term 网罗 [wǎng luó] referred to a net for catching both birds and animals.

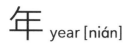 year [nián]

Oracle-bone   Bronze script   Small seal script

- This character's oracle bone script was a compound ideograph. It resembled a person going home with a sheaf of wheat on his back.
- 过年 [guò nián] *to celebrate the Spring Festival* is the last day of the year in which the ritual ceremony of ancestor worship was carried out, to bid farewell to the old and welcome the new.
- 同年 [tóng nián] not only referred to *being born in the same year*; it also meant *having passed the civil service examinations in the same year.*

华 magnificent, resplendent, prosperous [huá]

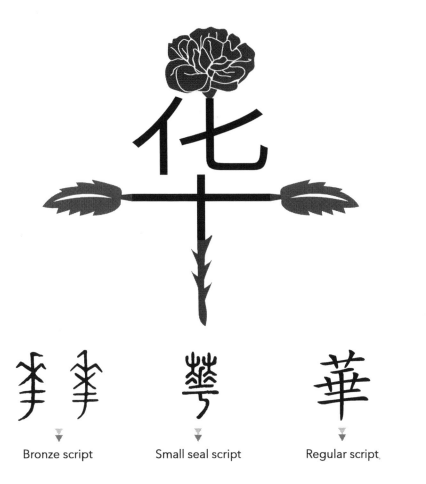

Bronze script | Small seal script | Regular script

- The metal script version of this character was a pictograph in the image of a flower, which was its original meaning.
- 华 denotes *flower*. As flowers come in different colors, hair that is the shade between black and white was known as 华发 [huá fà] *grey hair*.

休 to rest, to cease [xiū]

| Oracle-bone | Bronze script | Small seal script |

- This character is a compound ideograph. It resembled a person leaning against a tree to rest.
- In ancient times, the vacation system was called 休沐 [xiū mù] *official holiday on every fifth or tenth day of the month*. It provided the chance for officials to return home to rest and wash their hair.
- 致仕 [zhì shì] referred to the returning of an office to the emperor; 退休 [tuì xiū] means *to retire*.

朵 a quantitative term [duǒ]

Small seal script

Bronze script (颐)

Small seal script (颐)

- The small seal script for this character was the image of a flower facing downwards.
- 朵 could also denote the meaning of *two sides*. Therefore, the two buildings on each side of a main building were known as 朵楼 [duǒ lóu]. The right and left corridor of the audience hall in a palace or temple were known as 朵廊 [duǒ láng].
- The two terms 朵 and 颐 [yí] *cheek* could be used interchangeably to mean *cheeks swollen while chewing a big mouthful of food,* indicating that the food must be delicious.

 孝 filial piety [xiào]

Oracle-bone   Bronze script   Small seal script

- The oracle bone script for this character was a compound ideograph. It denoted a child holding an old man's hand, walking together.
- It is not clear whether the filial piety advocated by Confucianism means total obedience to parents.
- Humans practice filial piety. This behavior can be observed in animals too, hence the term 孝鸟 [xiào niǎo], literally meaning *filial bird* but extended to cover humans.

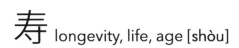 寿 longevity, life, age [shòu]

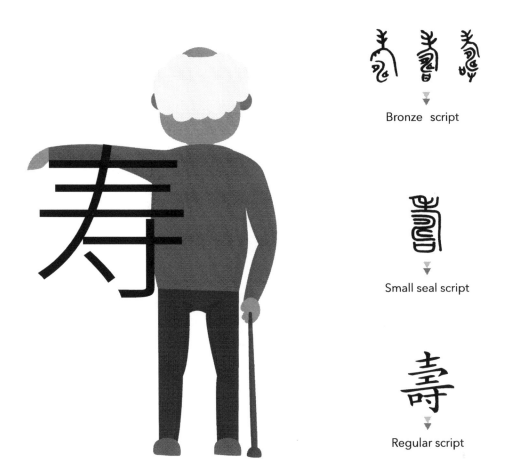

Bronze script

Small seal script

Regular script

- The five blessings in 五福临门 [wǔ fú lín mén] *well-wishes to bring five blessings upon the household* are 寿 *longevity*, 富 [fù] *wealth*, 康宁 [kāng níng] *good health*, 攸好德 [yōu hǎo dé] *virtue*, and 考终命 [kǎo zhōng mìng] *enjoyment of life until the end*.
- 寿 was a compound ideographic character in its metal script form. It resembled an old man doing farm work, indicating that doing physical work will result in a long life.
- People in ancient times divided a person's life span into three parts: 上寿 [shàng shòu] *advanced age*, 中寿 [zhōng shòu] *middle age*, and 下寿 [xià shòu] *age sixty*. Death after the age of eighty was considered a joyous occasion, and the funeral would be a celebration.

赤 red, loyal, sincere [chì]

| Oracle-bone | Bronze script | Small seal script |

- The oracle bone script for this character was a compound ideograph. It resembled a person cooking over a fire, indicating the color red.
- People in ancient times had to participate in a ritual ceremony to worship 赤帝 [chì dì] *the god of the south* on 立夏 [lì xià] *the beginning of summer (seventh solar term)*. This indicated that the heat of summer would soon arrive.
- 赤子 [chì zǐ] referred to a newborn baby, whose body would be red at birth.

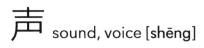 声 sound, voice [shēng]

Oracle-bone

Small seal script

Regular script

- 声 meant *the sound made by hitting stone chimes.*
- In ancient times, there was a great difference between 声 *sound*, 音 [yīn] *tone*, and 乐 [yuè] *music*. Animals could only differentiate sounds. Most people could only hear and understand tones. Only noblemen could understand music.
- From very early on, doctors of Traditional Chinese Medicine could diagnose ailments using the five sounds to correspond to the five internal organs.

戒 to guard against, to warn [jiè]

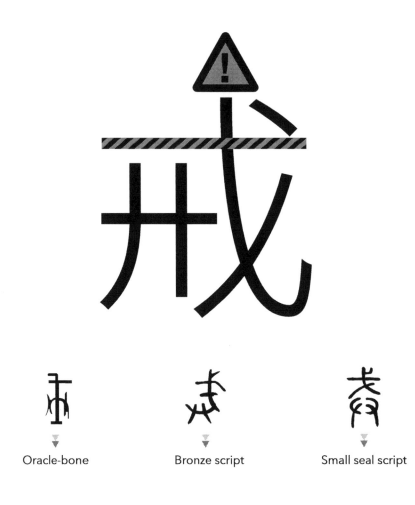

Oracle-bone   Bronze script   Small seal script

- This character's oracle bone form was a compound ideograph. It resembled two hands holding a dagger, indicating tight security.
- The original idea of the character was *alertness*.
- In the imperial palace, the emperor's concubines had 戒指 [jiè zhǐ] *rings* made of various materials, and wore them in different ways depending on whether they would be chosen as the emperor's bed partner, or whether they were pregnant.
- The most ceremonious 戒 in ancient China was the 斋戒 [zhāi jiè] *to abstain from meat and wine*. Before the ceremony, a bath and a change of clothes were required. The cleansing of the body was a display of reverence for the occasion.

巫 witch [wū]

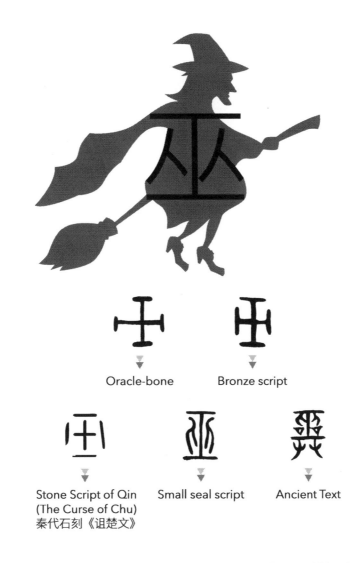

Oracle-bone   Bronze script

Stone Script of Qin
(The Curse of Chu)
秦代石刻《诅楚文》   Small seal script   Ancient Text

- The oracle bone script for this character was a pictograph. It could be described as the instrument used by a witch to perform acts of sorcery.
- A witch in ancient times was called 巫. Wizards were called 觋 [xí].
- A wizard's status was higher than that of a witch. Adding the radical 见 to the right of 巫 (觋) indicated the importance of this status.
- The phrase 小巫见大巫 [xiǎo wū jiàn dà wū] *to feel dwarfed in comparison* (literally - *a small sorcerer in the presence of a great one*) originated from *Zhuangzi*.

闲 to idle, leisure [xián]

Bronze script

Small seal script

Bronze script
(聞)

Small seal script
(聞)

- This is a compound ideographic character. The character's symbol resembled wood within a door, referring to a fence.
- The original character 间 [jiān] was written "閒", denoting the idea of peeping through a gap in a door to look at the moon. This is a compound ideograph, carrying the idea of a gap.
- Sunzi's *Art of War* divided 间谍 [jiàn dié] *spy* into five types. They were 因 [yīn] *the common people of an enemy country,* 内 [nèi] *an official in the enemy country,* 反 [fǎn] *the enemy's spy,* 死 [sǐ] *spies who sell false information to the enemy and are prepared to die,* and 生 [shēng] *spies who send back true information to their own country.*

我 I, me, myself [wǒ]

| Oracle-bone | Bronze script | Small seal script |

- The oracle bone script for this character was a pictograph of a military weapon.
- The military connotation of 我 meant that there was a notion of danger involved; thus, it was used as the first person pronoun.
- In ancient times, it was very rare for the term 我 to be used for addressing the self. The term 吾 [wú] was used instead.
- 余 [yú] and 吾 were both used for the self. However, the implication was different. 余 was more relaxed, but 吾 was haughty.

犹 like, similar to [yóu]

Oracle-bone

Bronze script

Small seal script

Regular script

- Both 犹 and 豫 [yù] were types of animal. 犹 was a type of monkey, and 豫 was a kind of ancient elephant.
- 豫 was a harmless elephant. This idea extended the character to mean *magnanimous*. It later became interchangeable with 娱 [yú] in the phrase 娱乐 [yú lè] *amusement, entertainment*.
- The two animals 犹 and 豫 had a common trait; they were both very suspicious. Subsequently, the characters were used to mean *indecisiveness*.

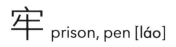 牢 prison, pen [láo]

Oracle-bone   Bronze script   Small seal script

- This character's oracle bone script was a compound ideograph. It was the image of a cow in a fenced area, denoting the idea of a pen.
- The phrase 牢骚 [láo sao] *complaint, grievance* arose from the grooms in the stable, as they grumbled while brushing the horses.
- 牢 referred to a pen to keep animals. It was extended to mean sacrificial offerings consisting of an ox, a sheep, and a pig, known as 太牢 [tài láo].

社 organized body, society, agency [shè]

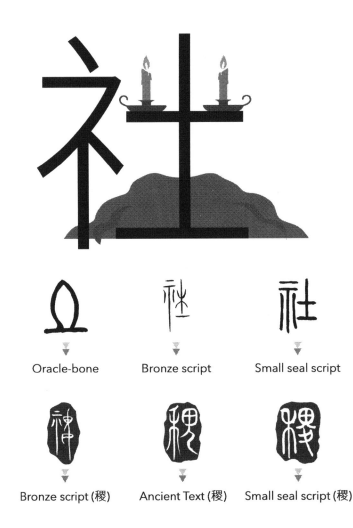

Oracle-bone   Bronze script   Small seal script

Bronze script (稷)   Ancient Text (稷)   Small seal script (稷)

- The oracle bone script for this character resembled a mound. It was later extended to refer to the sacrificial worship of the god of the soil.
- The modern-day phrases 社会 [shè huì] *society* and 社交 [shè jiāo] *social interactions* have their roots in ancient worship rites .
- Both 社 and 稷 [jì] *millet, or the god of grains* were affairs of the state. The ceremonies would often be held together. Subsequently, they evolved to mean *country*.

忍 to endure, to bear, to tolerate [rěn]

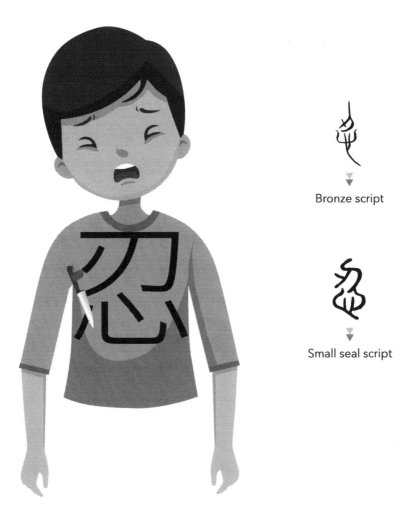

Bronze script

Small seal script

- Xu Shen, a Chinese scholar-official and philologist of the Eastern Han Dynasty, considered the character 忍 as a phonetic compound.
- It resembled a knife stabbed into a heart.
- The character encompassed both positive and negative implications. For example, whether one has the guts to kill another, or no guts to perform the act, both urges have to be controlled, i.e. 忍.

妻 wife [qī]

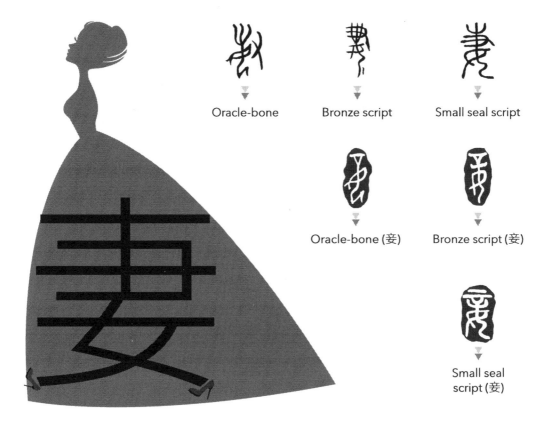

Oracle-bone

Bronze script

Small seal script

Oracle-bone (妾)

Bronze script (妾)

Small seal script (妾)

- Xu Shen, a Chinese scholar-official and philologist of the Eastern Han Dynasty, considered the character 妻 as a compound ideograph. It depicted a woman doing household chores.
- Some scholars regarded the character in its pictographic oracle bone script as the kidnapping of a bride, as marriage by abduction was practiced in ancient times.
- The term 妾 [qiè] *concubine* originally referred to a female slave who was guilty of breaking the law. Therefore, the character's symbol was a kneeling woman with an execution knife above her head.

丧 to lose, funeral, mourning [sàng]

Oracle-bone

Bronze script

Small seal script

Regular script

- The oracle bone script for this character was a phonetic compound. It had the radical of three mouths to represent weeping. In the middle was a mulberry tree to represent sounds.
- The original idea of 丧 was 丧失 [sàng shī] *lost*, as in 身丧 [shēn sàng] *when a person dies, his body will be gone.*
- In ancient times, there were five types of mourning clothes, ordered from the heaviest to the lightest. The first was 斩衰 [zhǎn shuāi] *a garment of unhemmed sackcloth*; followed by 齐衰 [qí shuāi] *the second thickest sackcloth, with the sides hemmed*; next was 大功 [dà gōng] *mourning clothes made from boiled linen*; after that was 小功 [xiǎo gōng] *the fourth in the order of mourning clothes*; and 缌麻 [sī má] *funeral clothing of the lightest degree.*

武 martial, military [wǔ]

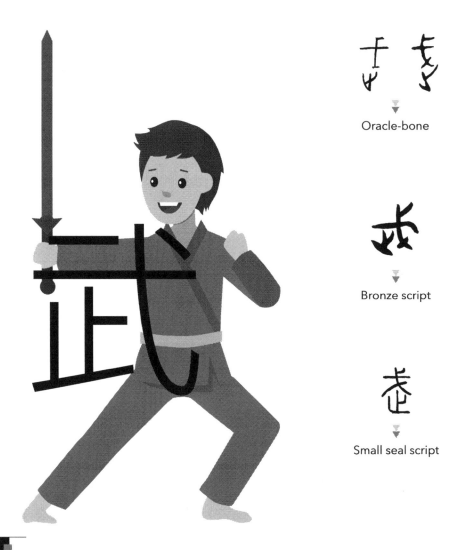

Oracle-bone

Bronze script

Small seal script

- The oracle bone script for this character was a compound ideograph. The character's symbol was a dagger with a person's foot below, indicating that they were armed and moving forward. Its meaning was *to use force*.
- King Zhuang of the feudal State of Chu explained that 武 meant that *military forces were only to be used to maintain peace and order*. Although this explanation did not correspond to the original idea behind 武, it was obvious that people in ancient times had reservations about war.
- 武 was also used as a unit for measuring measurement length. Six feet made one 步 [bù], and half of a 步 was one 武.

味 flavor, taste, smell [wèi]

Oracle-bone (未)

Bronze script (未)

Small seal script (未)

Small seal script

Seal script of Six Writings

- This character is a compound ideograph. The radical on the right was 未 [wèi] to represent 穗 [suì] *the ear of grain*, denoting the idea of tasting grain in the mouth.
- People in ancient times concluded that the five types of tastes were sourness, sweetness, bitterness, spiciness, and saltiness.
- Ancient people also believed that healthy eating had to match the seasons. The advice was to eat more sour food in spring, bitter food in summer, spicy food in autumn, and salty food in winter; food could be marinated with agents to make it more 滑 [huá] *smooth* and 甜 [tián] or 甘 [gān] (*sweet*).

贤 virtuous, worthy [xián]

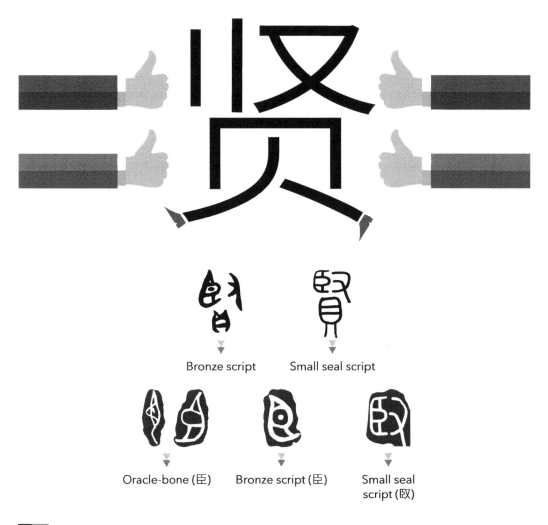

Bronze script   Small seal script

Oracle-bone (臣)   Bronze script (臣)   Small seal script (臤)

- This character's metal script form was a compound ideograph. It resembled a hand holding a slave, pushing him create more wealth. Therefore, the original idea behind this character was *more wealth*.
- The character 臣 [chén] in its oracle bone script form was a pictograph. It resembled an eye in a vertical form, to symbolize a male slave.
- The small seal script version of 臤 [qiān] *strong* was a compound ideograph, resembling a hand holding on to 臣 to imply *to hold firmly*.

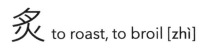 炙 to roast, to broil [zhì]

Small seal script   Ancient Text

- Roasting was very clearly defined in ancient times. 炮 [páo] was used to denote roasting meat with the hair still on it; 燔 [fán] was cooking meat with the hair removed; and 炙 was smoking meat with hair.
- The literal meaning of the phrase 亲炙 [qīn zhì] is *to be roasted in front of*. It was used to denote being tutored by somebody, or a teacher's instructions.

狐 fox [hú]

Oracle-bone   Small seal script

- The *Shuowen Jiezi Dictionary* defined the fox as an evil beast.
- According to legend, just before a fox died, its head would face its own lair. The phrase 狐死首丘 [hú sǐ shǒu qiū] meant *not to forget one's own origin*.
- People in ancient times discovered that the fox was a suspicious and mistrustful animal. The phrase 狐疑 [hú yí] *to be suspicious* has its roots in this knowledge.
- During the Tang Dynasty, it was a common practice to worship fox deities. There was even an idiom 无狐魅，不成村 [wú hú mèi, bù chéng cūn] *without a fox charm, there is no village.*

朋 friend [péng]

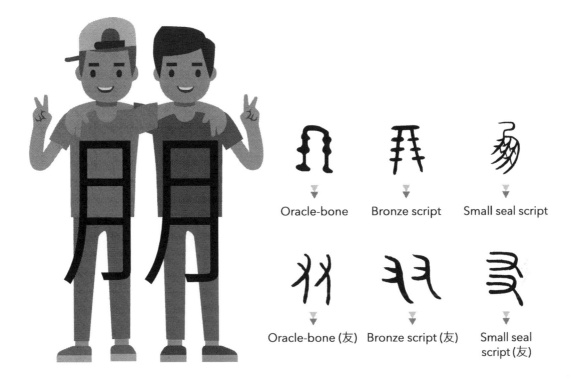

Oracle-bone   Bronze script   Small seal script

Oracle-bone (友)   Bronze script (友)   Small seal script (友)

- The oracle bone script for this character was a pictograph. It resembled two strings of cowrie shells tied together. Cowrie shells were used as currencies in ancient times.
- In early China, 朋 and 友 [yǒu] friend defined two different levels of friendship. Classmates or students learning from the same teacher could be regarded as 朋; only relationships among like-minded people could be called 友.
- Both 朋党 [péng dǎng] *clique*, and 朋比 [péng bǐ] *accomplice* have negative connotations.

岳 high mountain, wife's parents [yuè]

Oracle-bone   Small seal script

- The character 岳 is not a simplified form, but an ancient form of 嶽.
- The five mountains that 五岳 [wǔ yuè] depicted are Taishan in the east, Hengshan in Hunan in the south, Huashan in the west, Hengshan in Hebei in the north, and Songshan in the center. In earlier days, there were only four mountains. The central region was not on the list.
- The father-in-law of a man received the title 泰山 [tài shān] *Taishan*, as this mountain was the head of the five. He was called 岳父 [yuè fù], and his wife was 岳母 [yuè mǔ].

物 matter, thing [wù]

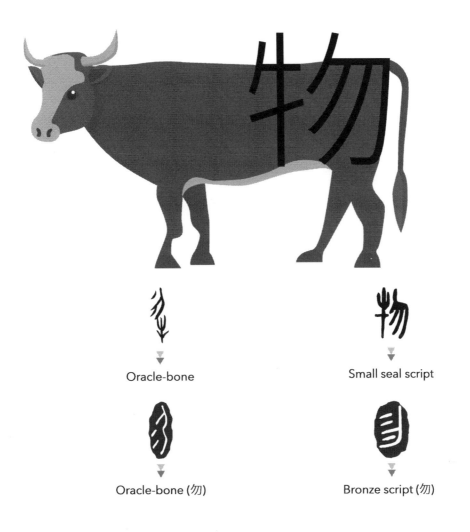

Oracle-bone

Small seal script

Oracle-bone (勿)

Bronze script (勿)

- This character used to mean *cattle that had more than one color*.
- 物 was related to 勿 [wù]. The latter denoted flags of more than one color. In ancient times, single-colored flags symbolized peace. Flags of more than one color denoted urgency. To get the common people to assemble quickly, a 勿 flag would be used.
- 物色 [wù sè] *to seek out* originally referred to the skin or fur of a domesticated animal. Therefore, 察物色 [chá wù sè] meant *to check the quality of the skin of animal sacrifices for worship rites*.

 treasure [bǎo]

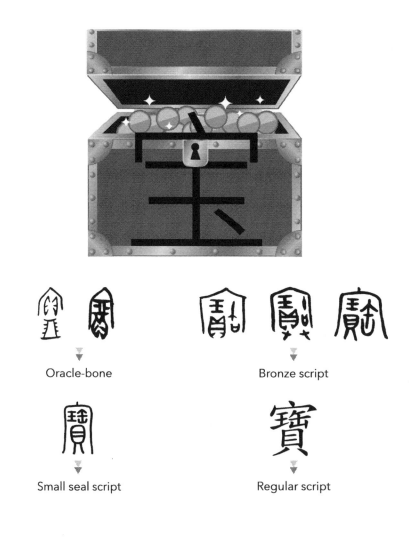

Oracle-bone

Bronze script

Small seal script

Regular script

- The oracle bone script for this character was a compound ideograph. Its symbol was a house with a shell and jade, denoting the idea of precious gems.
- As 宝 was very valuable, people in ancient times used it to denote respect, as in 宝位 [bǎo wèi] *the seat of a monarch* and 宝号 [bǎo hào] the polite way of saying *your shop*.
- The phrase 宝贝 [bǎo bèi] *treasured object* was used in ancient times to mean precious shells.

法 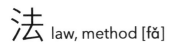 law, method [fǎ]

Bronze script   Small seal script   Regular script

— The ancient character for 法 was the very complex 灋. It denoted a 廌 [zhì] *a legendary animal*. This animal would use its horn to push out a person who was in the wrong, thus enforcing the law fairly.

— 廌 was also known as 獬豸 [xiè zhì] *a legendary animal that could distinguish good from evil, an upright mythical animal*. People in ancient times made hats in the image of this animal, to be worn by law enforcing judges.

柳 willow [liǔ]

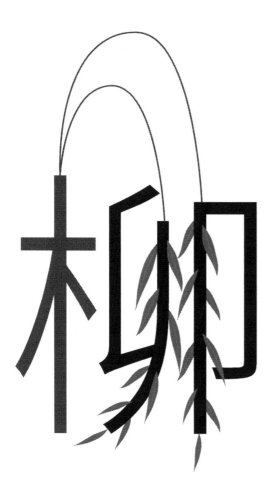

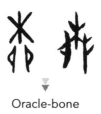

Oracle-bone

Bronze script

Small seal script

- The oracle bone script for this character was a pictograph. It resembled a bending willow branch.
- The characters 杨 [yáng] *poplar* and 柳 could be used together or used in place of each other. This is because 杨 is a type of 柳.
- 百步穿杨 [bǎi bù chuān yáng] *to hit a target at every shot* did not actually mean the poplar tree but the willow tree.
- As 柳 sounded similar to 留 [liú] *to stay,* 柳 was often used to imply sorrow at parting.

 冠 crown [guān] / crest [guàn]

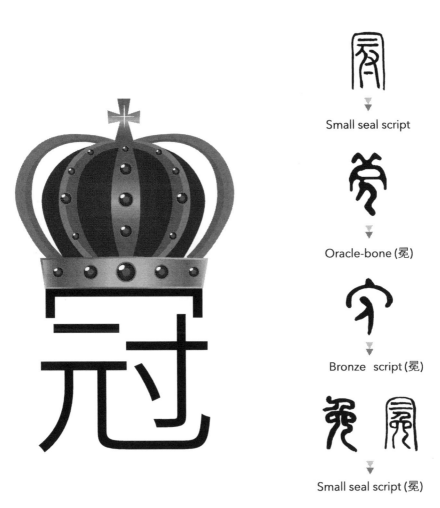

Small seal script

Oracle-bone (冕)

Bronze script (冕)

Small seal script (冕)

- The original idea of this character was a hat. As it was worn on the head, it implied being first.
- The character 冕 [miǎn] *crown* came from 免 [miǎn] *to avoid*. The oracle bone script for the latter was a pictograph and a compound ideograph. It resembled a kneeling person wearing a hat.
- 冠冕 [guān miǎn] *royal crown* was the headgear of the emperor and his government officials. This led to an extension of the meaning to denote *to be an official,* or *to be a leader.*

鬼 ghost, apparition [guǐ]

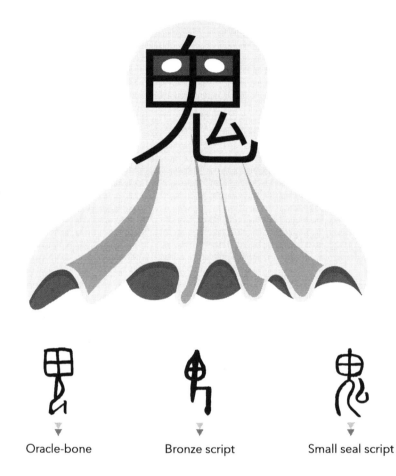

| Oracle-bone | Bronze script | Small seal script |

- The oracle bone script for this character was a pictograph. People in ancient times regarded a 鬼 as a large-headed person.
- The small seal script version of 鬼 had an additional radical 厶, to add horror to the image.
- People of old thought that there was a relation between 鬼 and 归 [guī] *to return*. They believed that the spirits of the dead would return to their homes.

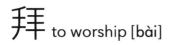 拜 to worship [bài]

Bronze script   Small seal script

— The metal script version of this character was a compound ideograph. Its symbol was a hand and a bowing person. The idea was raising one's hands above the head in worship.
— During the Zhou Dynasty, there were nine types of worship rites, known as 九拜 [jiǔ bài]. The first three were rites for joyous occasions; the six that followed were funeral rites.
— The practice of 膜拜 [mó bài] *to prostate oneself in worship,* was a Buddhist ritual, and a highly revered ceremonial rite. Long ago, it was used only for worshiping religious deities.

 autumn [qiū]

Oracle-bone

Large seal script

Small seal script

— This is a compound ideographic character. Its symbol resembled a tiny insect above a fire, indicating that grain was ready for harvest.
— According to the Five Elements, autumn belonged to the element of gold, a suitable time to carry out execution sentences. This idea was extended in phrases like 秋后问斩 [qiū hòu wèn zhǎn] *to be beheaded after the autumn harvest*, and 秋后算账 [qiū hòu suàn zhàng] *to settle accounts with somebody later*.
— In ancient times, the phrase 金秋 [jīn qiū] *golden fall* did not have the modern idea of beautiful autumn weather. It referred to the season when criminals on death row would be executed together.

俎 vessel used for sacrificial worship [zǔ]

Oracle-bone   Bronze script   Small seal script

- This character originally denoted the vessel for meat used in sacrificial worship. It was later extended to mean *a chopping board for cutting meat*.
- 刀俎 [dāo zǔ] denoted a butcher's knife and chopping board. 人为刀俎 [rén wéi dāo zǔ] means *to allow oneself to be oppressed and exploited*.
- 折冲樽俎 [zhé chōng zūn zǔ] refers to gaining victory not through force, but through negotiations over wine and feasting.

眉 eyebrow [méi]

Oracle-bone

Bronze script

Small seal script

- The oracle bone script for this character was a pictograph. It was an image of a large eye with hair above it.
- People in ancient times categorized the eyebrows as either delicate, thick, or fierce. The eyebrows were used as a way to assess a person's health.
- A woman's eyes are usually better looking than a man's; therefore 眉 was extended to mean *an attractive woman*.
- A moth is like a butterfly. Its antennae are long and curved. 蛾眉 [é méi] was derived from this image to denote a woman's beautiful eyebrows.

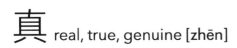 **真** real, true, genuine [zhēn]

Bronze script   Ancient Text   Small seal script

- This character is an ideogram, using four radicals 匕,目,乚,八 to indicate a 真人 [zhēn rén] *a perfect person*, who could rise up to heaven and become an immortal being.
- The radical 八 denoted the flying object that an immortal used. It could be a dragon, air, or a wheel.
- A 真人 had cultivated perfection and attained the Dao. 真was extended to refer to the sincerity and truthfulness of a person's nature and principles.

酌 to drink, to pour out, to consider [zhuó]

Bronze script

Small seal script

Small seal script (斟)

- On the left of the character 酌 was a wine vessel. On the right was a spoon with a long handle, implying that it was used to mix the wine.
- The small seal script for 斟 [zhēn] *to pour* was a phonetic compound. It meant *using a spoon to mix wine.*
- Both 斟 and 酌 mean *pouring wine*. The two were used interchangeably, leading to a new phrase 斟酌.

贼 thief, traitor [zéi]

Bronze script

Small seal script

Oracle-bone (盗)

Small seal script (盗)

- On the left of the metal script version of this character was a knife. On the right was a dagger above a shell, carrying the idea of using the dagger to damage the shell.
- The oracle bone script for 盗 [dào] was a compound ideograph, resembling a person drooling over a vessel filled with objects.
- In ancient times, 盗 and 贼 were used differently from their modern iterations. In the past, a person who stole was known as 盗, and one who robbed was 贼.

卿 a minister or a high official in ancient times [qīng]

Oracle-bone

Bronze script

Small seal script

– This character's symbol resembled two people feasting from a pot. Subsequently, the character was extended to mean *a person eating with a monarch*. Thus, 卿 became the term by which an emperor would address his ministers.

– 卿 could also be used between a married couple to express affection, as in 卿卿我我 [qīng qīng wǒ wǒ] *whispers of love*.

– According to ancient etiquette, 卿 was a term used by a person of a higher status to address someone of a lower status; a husband could use this term for his wife, but she could not use it in return.

臭 to smell [xiù] / smelly, foul, disgusting [chòu]

Oracle-bone · Seal script · Small seal script

- This is compound ideographic character. The top part, 自 [zì], was the symbol for a nose, and below it was 犬 [quǎn] *dog*, to denote using the nose to smell.
- 臭 was originally read as [xiù]. When used as a noun, it was a general term for *smell*. When used as a verb, it meant *to smell*.
- 其臭如兰 [qí xiù rú lán] was used to describe a fragrance that was as good as an orchid's.

朕 a term of self-address for a monarch [zhèn]

Oracle-bone

Bronze script

Small seal script

- The oracle bone script for this character was a compound ideograph, carrying the idea of holding a tool in one's hand to repair a boat. The original idea behind 朕 was *the joints of a boat*. Thus, it was extended to mean *crevice*.
- When 朕 was first used as self-address, anyone could adopt it.
- From the reign of the monarch Qin Shi Huang, only emperors could use this term to address themselves.

爱 love, affection [ài]

Bronze script   Small seal script

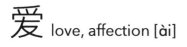

- The metal script version of this character was a compound ideograph. It resembled the action of handing one's heart to a loved one, carrying the idea of yearning for one's parents.
- The character was extended to cover many other things, including *closeness, grace, love of music,* and *frugality.*

家 home, family [jiā]

Oracle-bone

Bronze script

Small seal script

- This character is a compound ideograph comprising of the symbol for a house with a pig underneath it.
- In ancient times, the difference between the terms 国 [guó] *country* and 家 was that the former referred to the area governed by a monarch or dukes and princes, while the latter referred to the land allocated to the ministers.
- In ancient China, 国家 [guó jiā] *country* referred to "family under the sky" - the private property of an emperor.

宾 guest [bīn]

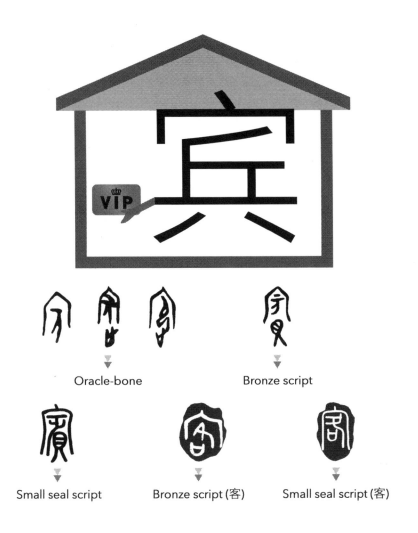

Oracle-bone

Bronze script

Small seal script

Bronze script (客)

Small seal script (客)

- In ancient times, there was a distinction between 宾 and 客 [kè] *guest*. The former was regarded as superior because it referred to important guests. The latter was considered of lesser value as it referred to guests of humble status.
- The oracle bone script for 宾 was a compound ideograph. Its symbol resembled a person walking into a house, denoting the idea of a visitor coming in.
- The metal script version of 客 was also a compound ideograph, denoting an outsider coming into a house.

 harm [hài]

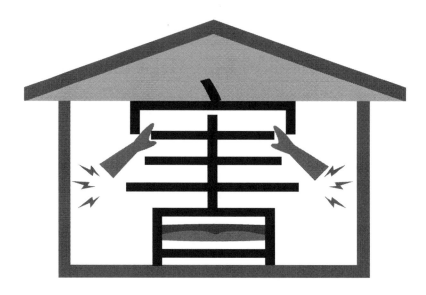

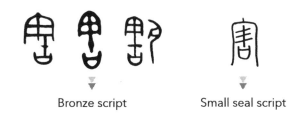

Bronze script   Small seal script

- This character is a compound ideogram, denoting the idea of harm brought about by a loose tongue.
- 害 can also be extended to mean *to bear the consequence of*, as in the phrases 害羞 [hài xiū] *be bashful*, and 害喜 [hài xǐ] *to suffer morning sickness when pregnant*.
- In the phrase 害群之马 [hài qún zhī mǎ] *one who brings disgrace to the community*, 害马 [hài mǎ] did not originally refer to a bad egg in a group, but things that could harm a horse.

酒 wine [jiǔ]

Oracle-bone

Bronze script

Small seal script

— On the right of the oracle bone script version of this character was the symbol of a wine vessel. On the left were droplets of wine.

— In ancient times, the drinking of wine was often prohibited when the food supply was insufficient. To avoid committing an offense, alternative euphemistic names like 圣人 [shèng rén], 贤人 [xián rén], 青州从事 [qīng zhōu cóng shì], and 平原都邮 [píng yuán dū yóu] were given to types of wine.

 to involve [shè]

Oracle-bone

Bronze script

Small seal script

- This character is a compound ideogram. In the middle is the image of a river, with a foot on each bank to denote crossing.
- 涉 was extended to cover the idea of perusing a book (as opposed to in-depth reading).
- The literal meaning of 涉猎 [shè liè] *cursory reading* is *to paddle into water, not knowing what is in it*; or *all eyes on the target animal while hunting, unaware of other details*. The idea behind this is a lack of focus.

羞 to be bashful, to be shy [xiū]

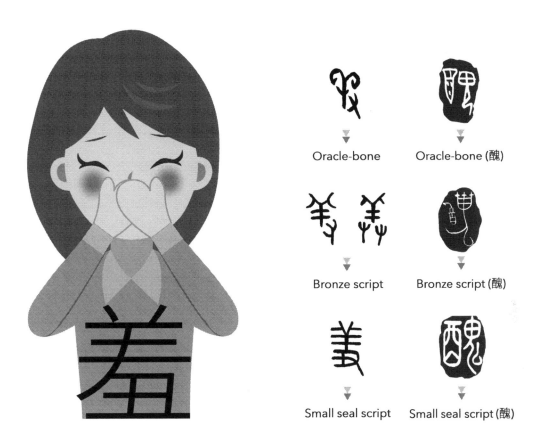

Oracle-bone

Oracle-bone (醜)

Bronze script

Bronze script (醜)

Small seal script

Small seal script (醜)

- 羞 is a compound ideograph made up of a hand holding a goat's head as an offering.
- People in ancient times added the radical 食 to this character to form 饈, referring to delicious food.
- The ancient pronunciation of 羞 was close to that of 丑 [chǒu], so the two became interchangeable, extending to 羞恥 [xiū chǐ] *a sense of shame*, and 害羞 [hài xiū] *to be bashful*.

祥 auspicious [xiáng]

Bronze script   Small seal script

- This character is a compound ideograph. It resembled a goat's head as an offering on the altar.
- In ancient times, all omens, whether good or bad, were regarded as 祥.
- The Book of Rites had rules for the two rites of 大祥 [dà xiáng] *a memorial ceremony at the end of the two-year period of mourning for a parent,* and 小祥 [xiǎo xiáng] *a memorial ceremony held at the end of the one-year period of mourning for a parent.*

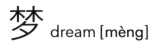

梦 dream [mèng]

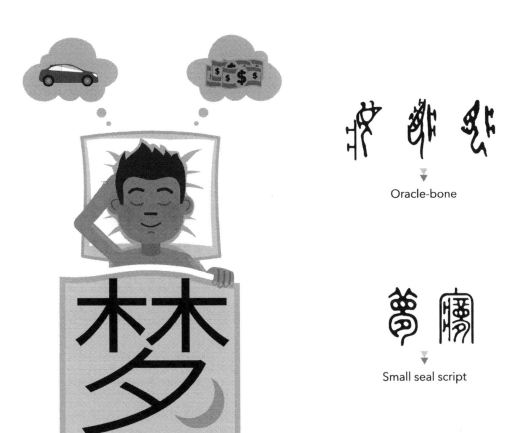

Oracle-bone

Small seal script

- The oracle bone script for this character was a compound ideograph. It resembled a person lying on a bed with his hand to his temple, to denote dreaming.
- People in ancient times viewed dreams seriously. During the Zhou Dynasty, there was an official position for a dream interpreter.
- Dreams were divided into six categories during the Zhou Dynasty, to determine whether they were auspicious or an inauspicious. These were 正梦 [zhèng mèng] *a dream during a peaceful sleep*, 噩梦 [è mèng] *a nightmare*, 思梦 [sī mèng] *to dream about something that had been on one's mind*, 寤梦 [wù mèng] *to see something during the day and dream about it at night*, 喜梦 [xǐ mèng] *to dream about something one was happy about*, and 惧梦 [jù mèng] *to dream about something one was fearful of*.

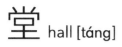 hall [táng]

| Bronze script | Small seal script |

- The idea behind this character was a very tall structure built on the ground.
- The image denoted the idea of grandeur and majesty, as in the phrases 相貌堂堂 [xiàng mào táng táng] *a dignified appearance*, and 堂皇 [táng huáng] *magnificent*.
- Ancient buildings were divided into three sections: 堂, 室 [shì] *the main house*, and 房 [fáng] *rooms*. The hall was at the front. The main function of this room was spirit worship. Behind the hall was the main house where the family lived. The rooms were at the two sides of the main house.

祭 offering [jì]

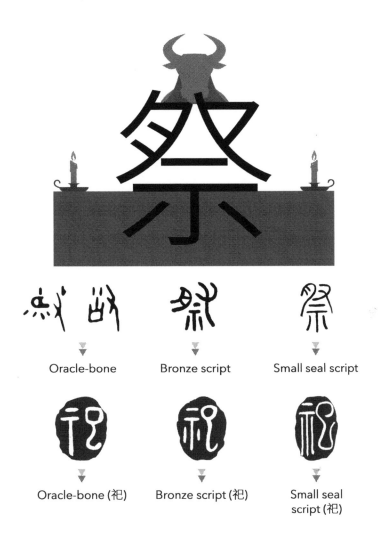

Oracle-bone   Bronze script   Small seal script

Oracle-bone (祀)   Bronze script (祀)   Small seal script (祀)

- This character is a compound ideograph showing a hand holding a piece of meat dripping with blood. It denotes the idea of a meat offering in sacrificial worship.
- 祀 [sì] is also a compound ideographic character, depicting a person kneeling at the altar, offering prayers.
- In ancient times, 祀 referred to the worship of the god of the heavens. It should not be confused with 祭, which was the worship of the god of the earth.

Bronze script   The Curse of Chu   Small seal script

- In ancient times, the character 婚 did not exist. Instead, 昏 [hūn] *dusk* was used, as wedding ceremonies were carried out in the evening.
- During ancient wedding ceremonies, the groom's family could not play music for three days and three nights. This was because when a son got married, it meant that his parents had reached old age. Therefore, there should not be too much fanfare.
- 婚 referred to "marrying off" a daughter. 姻 [yīn] *marriage*, on the other hand, was "marrying in" a daughter-in-law. When the two terms are used together, it becomes 婚姻 [hūn yīn] *marriage*.

族 family, clan, nationality, race [zú]

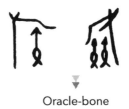

Oracle-bone

Bronze script

Small seal script

- 族 was the old form of 鏃. Its oracle bone script was a compound ideograph. On its left was a large flag, and below was an arrowhead pointing at it.
- In ancient times, fifty arrows were known as one 束 [shù] *bunch*. This idea extended the meaning of the character to *gather*. From this idea, it was extended further to *clan*.
- After all the extensions of 族 were exhausted, the character 鏃 was created to denote the original idea of 族.

望 to look over, to hope [wàng]

| Oracle-bone | Bronze script | Small seal script |

- This is a compound ideograph. The character's symbol resembled a person with two large eyes standing on a mound looking into the distance.
- There was an ancient ceremonial rite known as 望祭 [wàng jì], whereby emperors worshipped the mountains and rivers, the sun and moon, and the stars.
- 望 was extended and used in 名望 [míng wàng] *good reputation*. People with a good reputation would need to 仰望 [yǎng wàng] *look up to*, as in the phrase 德高望重 [dé gāo wàng zhòng] *to be of noble character and high prestige*.

雅 elegant [yǎ]

雅

Small seal script

- The character 雅 was the original character for 鸦 [yā] *crow*. The former was later used as a name for a wine vessel.
- 雅量 [yǎ liàng] initially referred to people who could hold alcohol very well.
- From the ability to hold alcohol, 雅 was later extended to mean *a good attitude towards wine drinking*. It eventually led to phrases such as 风雅 [fēng yǎ] *refined*, and 文雅 [wén yǎ] *polished*, to describe a cultured attitude.

 to bury [zàng]

Oracle-bone

Bronze script

Small seal script

Three Body Stone Classic 三体石经 (c. AD 220)

- This is a compound ideograph. Its symbol resembled a person lying in a coffin, denoting burial.
- In ancient times, burial ceremonies were very simple. A dead body was wrapped in a straw mat and buried in the wilderness.
- Before the Spring and Autumn Period, the system of burial was very simple. A grave was made by simply digging a hole in the ground, without a tombstone. If the grave was ever damaged, it would not be repaired.

落 fall, drop [luò]

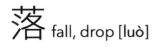
Small seal script

- 零 [líng] and 落 meant *to drop* or *to fall*. The former was used when describing grass withering and falling. The latter depicted the same situation for trees.
- In ancient times, after a building in the palace was completed, a sacrificial worship ceremony would be held. This ceremony was called 落, and it was extended to create the phrase 落成 [luò chéng] *completion*.

鼎 an ancient cooking vessel with three or four legs and two loop handles [dǐng]

Oracle-bone

Bronze script

Small seal script

- This is a pictographic character representing a three-legged cooking vessel with two loop handles.
- Da Yu (Yu the Great, a legendary ruler in ancient China) divided the land into nine administrative divisions, known as 九州 [jiǔ zhōu], which became another name for China. He also created nine 鼎 to represent these nine divisions. Subsequently, the meaning of 鼎 evolved from *a simple vessel for food* to become a symbol of the state's political power.
- The nine vessels belonged solely to a monarch. Therefore, to plot to take political power was known as 问鼎 [wèn dǐng].

 birds [qín]

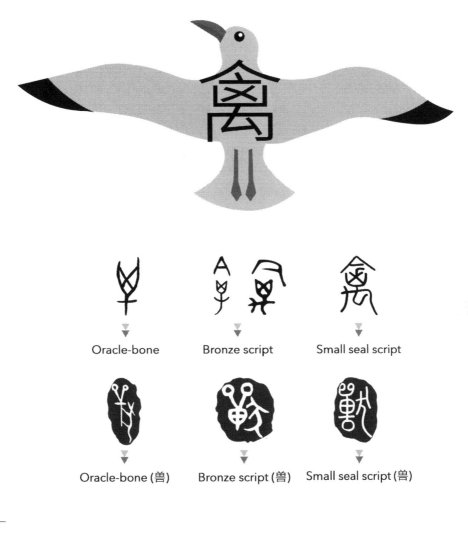

Oracle-bone   Bronze script   Small seal script

Oracle-bone (兽)   Bronze script (兽)   Small seal script (兽)

- The oracle bone script for this character was a pictograph resembling a net with a handle, denoting a tool for catching birds and beasts.
- 禽 referred to two-legged animals with feathers, and 兽 [shòu] referred to four-legged animals with fur or hair. Both were extensions of the original meaning.
- 兽 was a compound ideograph. On the left of the character was a tool for hunting, and on the right was a dog, to denote hunting.

 to honor, to respect, to revere [zūn]

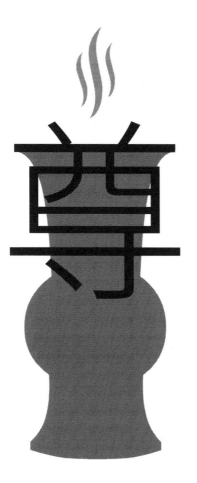

Oracle-bone

Bronze script

Small seal script

- This is a pictographic character meaning *a wine vessel*.
- Toasting with wine is a display of respect. Therefore, 尊 was later extended to mean *to show respect*. The original idea of a wine vessel was replaced by 罇 [zūn], 樽 [zūn], and other similar terms.

禄 prosperity [lù]

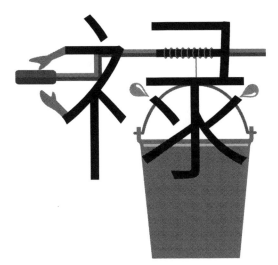

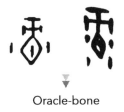 

Oracle-bone   Bronze script   Small seal script

- 禄 is a compound ideograph. The character's symbol resembled a pulley letting down a bucket into a well, splashing water everywhere. The image denoted a catchment area for irrigation to ensure a bountiful harvest.
- Initially there was no distinction between 福 [fú] *blessings* and 禄. The latter was eventually used to mean *salary for government officials*. The former was then used to mean *good fortune* and *good luck*.
- In ancient times, the death of a scholar was known as 不禄 [bù lù], meaning that he did not have the good fortune to continue holding his official position.

禅 Zen, deep meditation [chán] / to abdicate the throne [shàn]

Small seal script

Seal Script

– 禅 was originally used as 墠 [shàn], referring to land that had been cleared of grass and weeds. Subsequently, to deify the character, the radical 土 was replaced by 示, to denote a form of worship.

– When 禅 was read as [chán], it denoted matters pertaining to Buddhism.

– When read as [shàn], it referred to worship of the earth in ancient times.

善 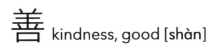 kindness, good [shàn]

Oracle-bone

Bronze script

Small seal script

Small seal script (恶)

- This is a compound ideograph. The character's symbol was a goat with two 言 radicals below it, to denote the subject as auspicious and good.
- According to Xu Sheng's explanation in the *Shuowen Jiezi Dictionary,* 善 was a phonetic compound, with 心 [xīn] as its semantic part, and 亚 [yà] as its phonetic radical. Many scholars have noted that the character 亚 resembled the plan of an underground tomb during the Yin Dynasty.

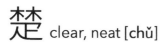 clear, neat [chǔ]

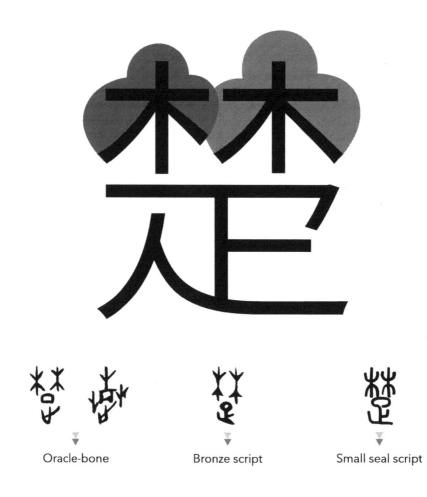

Oracle-bone   Bronze script   Small seal script

– This is a compound ideograph. It comprises of two trees above a foot, denoting deforestation for development.

– The people of the State of Chu held the title 楚 because their dwelling area mainly consisted of forests that needed to be developed. They were called 楚人 [chǔ rén], and the state was called 楚国 [chǔ guó].

– 楚木 [chǔ mù] *a type of shrub* was taller than most shrubs. Thus, 楚楚 [chǔ chǔ] was extended to mean *bright and clear*, as in the phrase 衣冠楚楚 [yī guān chǔ chǔ] *in smart clothes.*

 thunder [léi]

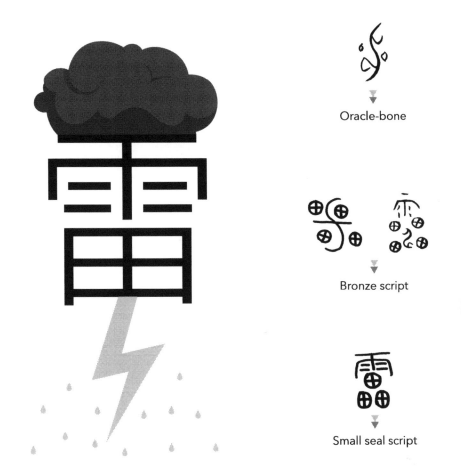

Oracle-bone

Bronze script

Small seal script

- This character is a pictograph. The symbol for lightning is in the middle, and the circles on both sides represent the sound of thunder.
- People in ancient times believed that the sound of thunder could be heard a hundred miles away. The character 同 [tóng] was a unit of land in those days, covering an area of a hundred miles. The meaning of 雷同 [léi tóng] *identical* was the result of combining the two characters.
- The phrase 五雷 [wǔ léi] in 五雷轰顶 [wǔ léi hōng dǐng] *to be thunderstruck, to suffer a heavy blow* refers to the Thunder God's five brothers.

蜀 another name for Sichuan province [shǔ]

Oracle-bone Bronze script Small seal script

- This is a pictographic character. It resembles a worm with a huge eye, and refers to a silkworm.
- Sichuan is also known as 蜀. During the State of Shu, sericulture was a major farming activity.
- The literal meaning of 蜀犬吠日 [shǔ quǎn fèi rì] *astonishment at an unfamiliar sight* was 'dogs barking at the sun'. This is because the sun was a rare sight, as it was often foggy in the State of Shu. Therefore, things that were seldom seen were strange.

罪 guilt, fault, misconduct [zuì]

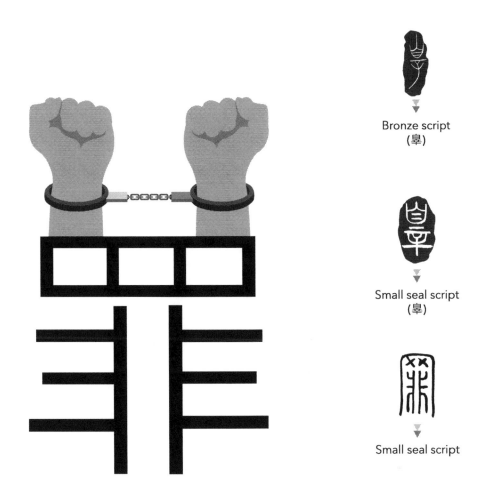

Bronze script
(辠)

Small seal script
(辠)

Small seal script

- The original character for 罪 was 辠. It was a compound ideograph. The image of an execution knife and a nose denoted suffering while serving a prison term.
- The ideograph of 罪 was a net and a bird with open wings, referring to the bamboo net used for catching fish and birds.
- Qin Shi Huang (the founding emperor of the Qin Dynasty) decided that the character 辠 was too similar to the character 皇 [huáng] *emperor*, and ordered that 罪 be used to replace 辠.

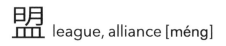 league, alliance [méng]

Oracle-bone   Bronze script   Small seal script

- This character is a compound ideograph. It resembles a plate with items for sacrificial worship, which were used to pledge alliance in the presence of the divine beings.
- During the pledging ritual, the host of the ceremony would hold a plate of ox's ears, known as 执牛耳 [zhí niú ěr] *the acknowledged leader*. This brought forth the idea that a person could occupy a leading position in certain areas.
- The phrase 歃血 [shà xuè] in 歃血为盟 [shà xuè wéi méng] *to smear blood as a sign of an oath* referred to drinking a tiny sip of the blood, or being dipped in blood, to show both parties' sincerity.

鉴 warning, to inspect [jiàn]

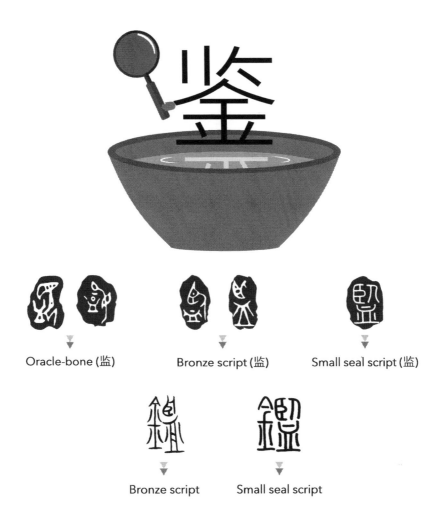

Oracle-bone (監)   Bronze script (監)   Small seal script (監)

Bronze script   Small seal script

- 監 [jiān] was the original character for 鉴. The character's oracle bone script version was a person kneeling in front of a basin to look at himself, to imply observing oneself in a mirror.
- According to legend, Qin Shi Huang (the founding emperor of the Qin Dynasty) had a mirror that could tell whether a person had evil intent. A plaque with the phrase 秦镜高悬 [qín jìng gāo xuán] *the mirror of Qin hung high – perspicacious decisions on criminal judgement* was later hung in the hall. The phrase was eventually changed to 明镜高悬 [míng jìng gāo xuán] *a bright mirror hung high – a fair and just judge.*

鼠 mouse, rat [shǔ]

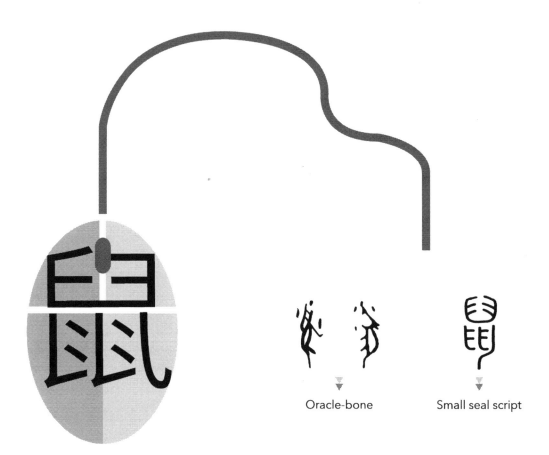

Oracle-bone

Small seal script

- This is a pictographic character. Its symbol had all the features of a mouse, with a belly, claws, tail, mouth, and protruding teeth.
- People in ancient times disliked rats, so this character was often used together with thievery, as in the phrase 鼠窃狗盗 [shǔ qiè gǒu dào] *petty thieves and small-time robbers.*
- Another name for a rat is 耗子 [hào zi]. It was derived from the common people's hatred of exorbitant taxes and levies.

解 to separate, to divide, solution [jiě]

Oracle-bone	Bronze script	Small seal script

- This is a compound ideograph. The character's symbol resembled a hand breaking off the horns of an ox, denoting the idea of dissecting the beast with a knife.
- The original meaning of 解手 [jiě shǒu] was *to break off a relationship*. It was later changed to mean *going to the toilet*.
- 解 included the idea of giving away the horn that was cut off. Therefore, it was extended to mean *to send out,* or *to escort*. When used in this context, it is read in its fourth tone [jiè], as in 押解 [yā jiè] *to send away under escort*, and 解差 [jiè chāi] *guards escorting prisoners*.

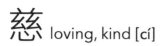 慈 loving, kind [cí]

Bronze script

Small seal script

Seal Script

- This is a compound ideographic character, resembling a heart with plants growing on it, to denote nurturing one's children with love.
- In the *Book of Etiquettes and Rites* during the Zhou Dynasty, the term 慈母 [cí mǔ] *a loving mother* did not refer to a biological mother, but to a foster mother who brought the child up.
- The word 慈 did not originally refer to a mother. It was only when the standard for 五常 [wǔ cháng] *the five cardinal relationships* was established that the idea of 父严母慈 [fù yán mǔ cí] *a strict father and a benevolent mother* became a social expectation.

 舞 to dance [wǔ]

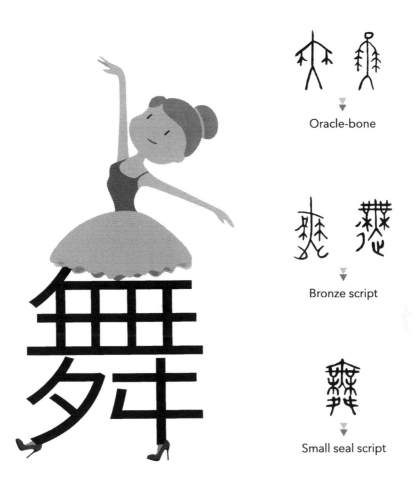

Oracle-bone

Bronze script

Small seal script

- This is a pictographic character, resembling a person holding the tail of an ox as if dancing.
- People in ancient times held dancing in high regard. During the Zhou Dynasty, dance was a subject that children had to learn. This was taught by professional musicians.
- When dancing, one's body had to move. Thus, 舞 was extended to mean *to dally with*, as in the phrase 舞弊 [wǔ bì] *malpractice*.

鲜 delicious, fresh, bright [xiān]

Bronze script

Small seal script

Bronze script (鱻)

Small seal script (鱻)

- The original character for 鲜 was 鱻, denoting the idea of making a dish with a fish that was still fresh.
- Although the character's symbols were later replaced by the semantics 鱼 [yú] *fish* and 羊 [yáng] *sheep*, it did not mean that cooking fish and sheep together in a pot would result in 鲜. The semantic 羊 was added to represent tastiness.
- 鲜 was extended to mean 新鲜 [xīn xiān] *fresh*. 明丽 [míng lì] *bright and beautiful* was used for anything related to taste and accessories.

德 virtue, morals [dé]

Oracle-bone

Bronze script

Small seal script

- This character is a compound ideograph, resembling a person walking slowly, looking straight ahead.
- The original idea of 德 was 升 [shēng], meaning *to ascend*. One had to continue working hard on one's 德性 [dé xìng] *moral character* to achieve ascension. This idea was extended to the phrase 德行 [dé xíng] *moral conduct*.
- 德配 [dé pèi] *a virtuous wife* was used to address another person's wife respectfully in her obituary.

 器 utensil [qì]

Bronze script

Small seal script

- This character's small seal script was a compound ideograph. It resembled a dog with four 口 radicals around it, depicting many objects. The dog was sent to guard them.
- The original idea of 器 was *a utensil*. It was later extended to denote valuable items, such as 神器 [shén qì] *the imperial stamp representing political power*, 宝器 [bǎo qì] *treasure*, and 大器 [dà qì] *treasure, or people with talents*.
- Due to the value of 器, it was frequently used to refer to people with great talents, like 大器晚成 [dà qì wǎn chéng] *a great man becoming famous late in life*.

儒 a scholar of Confucianism [rú]

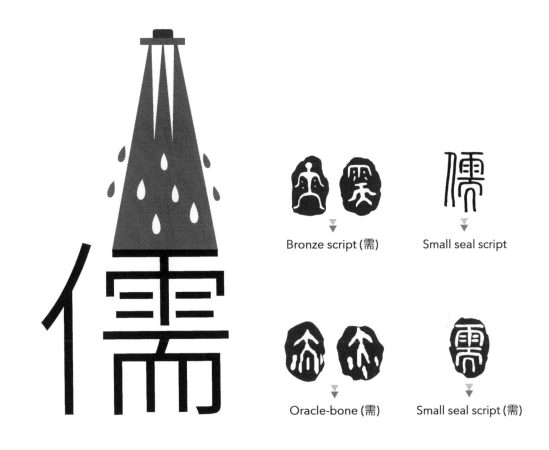

Bronze script (需)

Small seal script

Oracle-bone (需)

Small seal script (需)

- When 儒 was used as 濡 [rú] *to immerse*, it carried the idea of being moistened, to use the first emperor's methods of irrigating the bodily system.
- Hu Shi, a Chinese leader and scholar, explained that the earliest group of 儒 referred to survivors from the period of Yin Shang, who held jobs in the area of divination. During the Eastern Zhou Dynasty and the Spring and Autumn Period, this group of people switched to jobs in the performance of funeral rites.

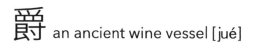 **爵** an ancient wine vessel [jué]

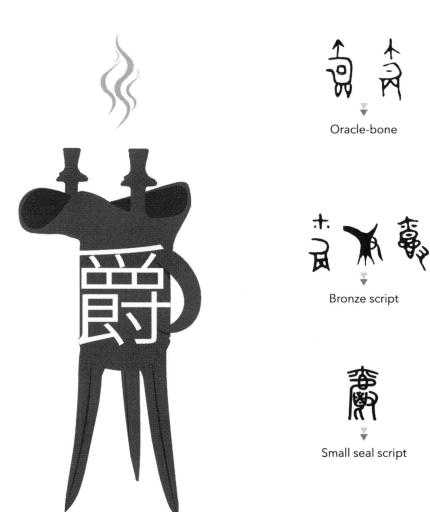

Oracle-bone

Bronze script

Small seal script

- 爵 and 雀 [què] *sparrow* were used interchangeably. 爵 was a sparrow-shaped wine vessel.
- 爵 was a sacrificial vessel used during worship and feasting. It was eventually extended to mean *a title of nobility*.
- Making wine vessels in the shape of a sparrow functioned to remind the user to control his drinking. The chirping of a sparrow sounded like a word of advice to stop once sated.

Small seal script

Seal Script

— The old version of 羹 carried the idea of cooking lamb over an ancient tripod to make a tasty dish.

— The original idea of this character was *juicy meat*. After the Wei-Jin Period, 羹 began to refer to meat soup.

— 闭门羹 [bì mén gēng] *cold shoulder treatment* initially meant *the refusal of prostitutes to accept guests.*

囊 bag, pocket, anything shaped like a bag [náng]

Small seal script

- 囊 referred to a bag. Phrases that derived from this idea were 智囊 [zhì náng] *a wise man*, 囊括 [náng kuò] *to include*, and 囊中之物 [náng zhōng zhī wù] *certain of attainment*.
- Derived from the 'Seven Bamboo Sages' of the Eastern Jin Dynasty, the term 阮囊羞涩 [ruǎn náng xiū sè] means *insufficient funds to meet necessary expenses*.

饕 covetous [tāo]

Bronze script

Small seal script

Small seal script (餮)

Large seal script

- Both 饕 and 餮 [tiè] mean *greedy*. The former referred to greed for wealth, and the latter referred to greed for food, or gluttony.
- 饕餮 was the name of one of the nine sons of the legendary Dragon – the one who loved food.
- People in ancient times carved 饕餮 on cooking vessels to remind people not to over-indulge in food and die from over-eating.

BIO OF XU HUI

Born in 1969, Xu Hui is a freelance writer, presently residing in Dali, Yunnan. He was the chief editor for *Temperament of the Sixties, The Backdoor of Chinese History*, and other works, and co-author of *The New Shuowen Interpretation, The Chinese Language Dictionary*, and the series *Looking at History the Fun Way*. His books include *The Art of Body Charm: Body Politics in Chinese History, Troubled Times Specimens: Personality Disorder in Chinese History, The Whip of Troubled Times: Thirty Most Controversial People in Chinese History, The Most Misunderstood Idioms of the Chinese People*, and *Enlightening Interpretation of Chinese Phrases*.

BIO OF JULIE LOO

Julie Loo, a former principal of Shanghai Singapore International School, Xuhui Campus, has been in the education field in Singapore and Shanghai for more than 28 years. Being an educator, she shares the author's passion in wanting people learning Chinese Language to appreciate the beauty of the language.